GOD'S GRACIOUS GIFT OF ASSURANCE

COMPACT EXPOSITORY PULPIT COMMENTARY SERIES

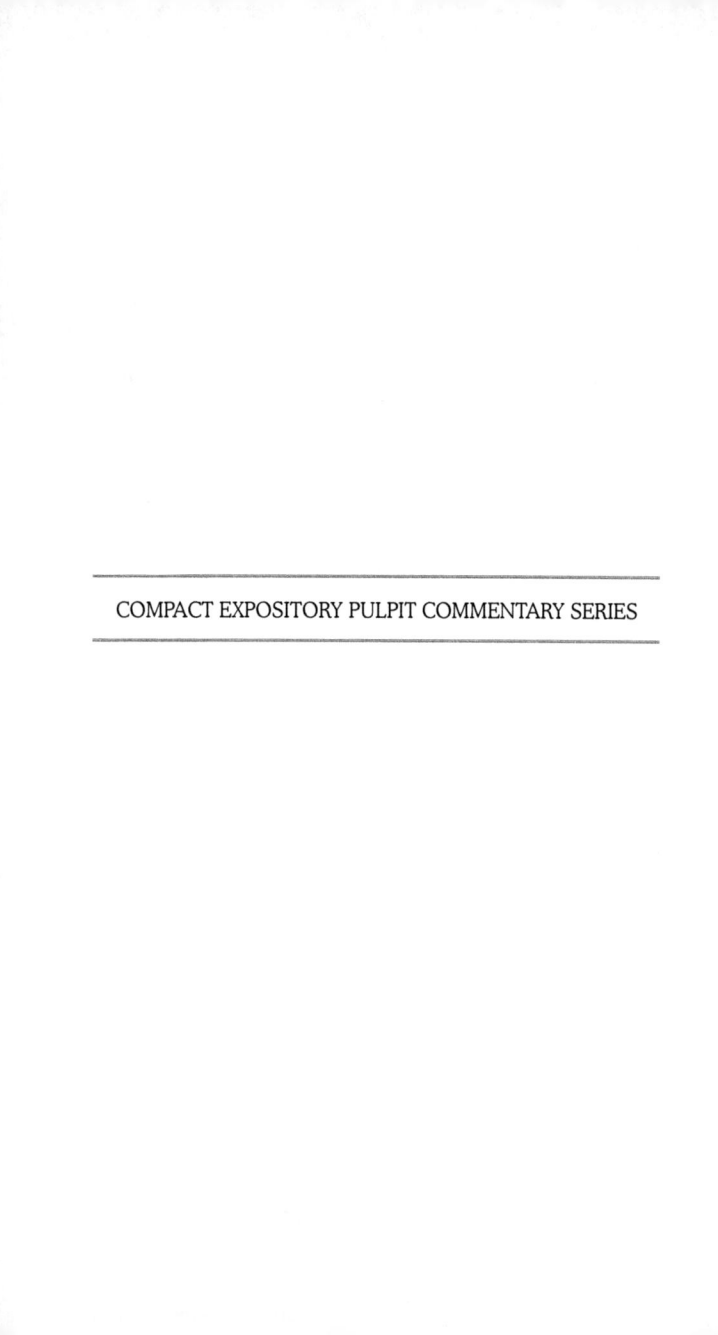

GOD'S GRACIOUS GIFT OF ASSURANCE

Rediscovering the Benefits of
Justification by Faith

DAVID A. HARRELL

© 2019 David A. Harrell

ISBN 978-1-7343452-1-6

Great Writing Publications, 425 Roberts Road, Taylors, SC 29687 www.greatwriting.org

Shepherd's Fire 5245 Highway 41-A Joelton, TN 37080 www.shepherdsfire.com

All Scripture quotations, unless stated otherwise, are taken from the New American Standard Bible® (NASB), Copyright © 1960, 1962, 1963, 1968, 1971, 1972, 1973, 1975, 1977, 1995 by The Lockman Foundation. Used by permission. www.Lockman. org All rights reserved.

No part of this publication may be reproduced, or stored in a retrieval system, or transmitted, in any form or by any means, mechanical, electronic, photocopying, recording or otherwise, without the prior permission of the publishers.

Shepherd's Fire exists to proclaim the unsearchable riches of Christ through mass communications for the teaching ministry of Bible expositor David Harrell, with a special emphasis in encouraging and strengthening pastors and church leaders.

Table of Contents

Books in this Series 6

Introduction 7

Peace with God 14

Access to God 29

A Permanent Standing Before God 41

A Jubilant Hope of Glory 54

Joy in Tribulation 65

Proof of Salvation 73

Hope through a Subjective Awareness of God's Love 84

Endnotes 95

Books in this Series

Finding Grace in Sorrow: Enduring Trials with the Joy of the Holy Spirit

Finding Strength in Weakness: Drawing Upon the Existing Grace Within

Glorifying God in Your Body: Seeing Ourselves from God's Perspective

God, Evil, and Suffering: Understanding God's Role in Tragedies and Atrocities

God's Gracious Gift of Assurance: Rediscovering the Benefits of Justification by Faith

Our Sin and the Savior: Understanding the Need for Renewing and Sanctifying Grace

The Marvel of Being in Christ: Adoring God's Loving Provision of New Life in the Spirit

The Miracle of Spiritual Sight: Affirming the Transforming Doctrine of Regeneration

Introduction

There is no greater source of joy in the life of a Christian than knowing that he or she has been reconciled to God through faith in His Son, our Substitute and Surety, the Lord Jesus Christ. To know that our sins are forgiven and the merits of Jesus are now ours through imputation—solely as a gift of God's grace—produces such soul-satisfying kinship with our Creator that all fears of standing before His holy tribunal evaporate like a morning mist before the sun. Herein is the heart of the doctrine of justification—a doctrine that many believers only appreciate and enjoy superficially.

While sin, doctrinal error, and ignorance can rob a believer of the life-sustaining blessings that flow from the fountain of grace, I fear the greatest culprit may well be the relentless distractions of life that can prevent us from habitually meditating upon the life-giving truths of the gospel. Whether it's smart phones or television, kids' sports or even church activities, it seems as though there is always a host of bandits stealing our attention and affections. Instead of setting our minds on things above, we focus on the things of this earth. Perhaps you find yourself in this category, as I do from time to time.

It has been my experience that when this happens, a strange numbing of the conscience begins to justify our trivial (and often sinful) pursuits, producing within us a quiet lethargy of spirit that douses our love for Christ with the waters of a lukewarm religion—a tragic condition that now characterizes much of evangelicalism.

But I have also discovered that in these seasons of apathy, God will often use some form of darkness to make us appreciate light—His light. Such is the case with a very dark article in *The Atlantic* that caught my eye entitled, "Three Decades Ago, America Lost Its Religion. Why?" What struck me most was not so much the worldly speculations used to explain why America has "lost its religion," but the sad testimony of the author who obviously knows nothing of his sin or the soul-exhilarating joy of being reconciled to an infinitely holy God through faith in Jesus Christ. The following is a quote that illustrates how God can use the darkness of deception to contrast the glorious light of truth.

The deeper question is whether the sudden loss of religion has social consequences for Americans who opt out. Secular Americans, who are familiar with the ways that traditional faiths have betrayed modern liberalism, may not have examined how organized religion has historically offered solutions to their modern existential anxieties. Making friends as an adult without a weekly congregation is hard. Establishing a weekend routine to soothe Sunday-afternoon nerves is hard. Reconciling the overwhelming sense of life's importance with the universe's ostensible indifference to human suffering is hard. Although belief in God is no panacea for these problems, religion is more than a theism. It is a bundle: a theory of the world, a community, a social identity, a means of finding peace and purpose, and a weekly routine. Those, like me, who have largely rejected this package deal, often find themselves shopping à la carte for meaning, community, and routine to fill a faith-shaped void. Their politics is a religion. Their work is a religion. Their spin class is a church. And not looking at their phone for several consecutive hours is a Sabbath. American nones (Americans who say they do not associate with any established religion) may well build successful secular systems of belief, purpose, and community. But imagine what a devout believer might think: Millions of Americans have abandoned religion, only to re-create it everywhere they look.[1]

The author's dark perspective unwittingly describes what God calls *idolatry*—that which man creates "to fill a faith-shaped void." Jonathan Edwards defined it biblically this way:

> Man will necessarily have something that he respects as his god. If man do not give his highest respect to the God that made him, there will be something else that has the possession of it. Men will either worship the true God, or some idol: it is impossible it should be otherwise: something will have the heart of man. And that which a man gives his heart to, may be called his god: and therefore when man by the fall extinguished all love to the true God, he set up the creature in his room. For having lost his esteem and love of the true God, and set up other gods in his room, and in opposition to him; and God still demanding their worship, and opposing them; enmity necessarily follows.[2]

Before coming to faith in Christ, we were all rebellious idolaters. We were all under the sentence of God's curse upon sin. But because of His unmerited grace, we have "been justified by faith" and we now "have peace with God through our Lord Jesus Christ, through whom also we have obtained our introduction by faith into this grace in which we stand; and we exult in hope of the glory of God" (Rom. 5:1-2). This is "the light of the gospel of the glory of Christ" (2 Cor. 4:4), "the light of the knowledge of the glory of God in the face of Christ" (v. 6). And these are the astounding truths upon which we must continually meditate and apply to our lives for our good and His glory.

One of the greatest measures of genuine saving faith is a believer's sincere gratitude for what God has done on his or her behalf. A mature believer will live in a state of boundless adoration and often express the sentiment of the apostle Paul who declared, "Thanks be to God for His indescribable gift!" (2 Cor. 9:15). And at the heart of that gift is the magnificent doctrine of justification by faith alone. Paul declared that people are justified solely because of God's grace through faith, and not of works. We are "justified as a gift by his grace" (Rom. 3:24) and with that justification come at least seven astounding benefits we can enjoy as we understand them and apply them to our lives.

Simply stated, *justification is that divine gift whereby God, through His grace, imputes the righteousness of Christ to believers, declares them to be righteous, and then treats them as such.* This transforming gift is not merely some initial blessing that stands alone. Rather, it is a blessing that encompasses all God gives the redeemed. Justification impacts every area of our life. It is the bedrock upon which our salvation is permanently and immovably anchored.

The focus of this mini-book will be to explain and apply these seven benefits as they are expressed in Romans 5. We have:

- Peace with God;
- Access to God;
- A Permanent Standing Before God;
- Jubilant Hope of Glory;
- Joy in Tribulation;
- Proof of Salvation;
- Hope Through a Subjective Awareness of God's Love.

My desire is for every believer to know and apply these truths to their life, and as a result, to enjoy an unshakable blessed assurance of eternal salvation, and experience the fullness of joy in Christ available to us this side of glory. Paul's prayer for the saints in Ephesus perfectly summarizes my passion:

> That He would grant you, according to the riches of His glory, to be strengthened with power through His Spirit in the inner man; so that Christ may dwell in your hearts through faith; and that you, being rooted and grounded in love, may be able to comprehend with all the saints what is the breadth and length and height and depth, and to know the love of Christ which surpasses knowledge, that you may be filled up to all the fullness of God (Eph. 3:16-19).

1

Peace with God

*Therefore, having been justified by faith,
we have peace with God through our Lord Jesus Christ.*
ROMANS 5:1

Because man is a sinner by nature, he has rebelled against our Holy God and is therefore at war with Him. However, apart from the convicting and regenerating power of the Holy Spirit, he will never see his situation. God's Word is clear: "The mind set on the flesh is hostile toward God; for it does not subject itself to the law of God, for it is not even able to do so, and those who are in the flesh cannot please God" (Rom. 8:7). The unregenerate

> walk in the futility of their mind, being darkened in their understanding, excluded from the life of God, because of the ignorance that

is in them, because of the hardness of their heart; and they, having become callous, have given themselves over to sensuality, for the practice of every kind of impurity with greediness (Eph. 4:17-19).

Because of his innate depravity man is ruled by his flesh and enslaved by his sin. He is a friend of the world, and friendship of the world is "enmity with God" (James 4:4). For this reason, the wrath of God abides upon the ungodly who have violated His law and who reject His gracious provision of forgiveness and reconciliation through faith in the Person and Work of His beloved Son, the Lord Jesus Christ (John 3:36).

When someone comes to realize that he is in a state of sedition against his Creator who holds the keys to heaven and hell and whose wrath endures forever, sheer terror will seize his heart. He will be like Belshazzar whose knees knocked together in abject horror when he saw the hand writing of judgment appear on the walls of his palace declaring the divine verdict: "'TEKĒL'—you have been weighed on the scales and found deficient" (Dan. 5:27).

By nature, however, man is incapable of seeing the true condition of his soul before a holy God. He will compare himself to others and be convinced of his superior righteousness. He will always be just in his own eyes. He will be at peace with himself, but not with God. He will live under the delusion that his good works will sufficiently impress God and be the grounds for his admittance into heaven. But, in fact, he has laid his spiritual foundation on sand, and fails to consider what is written, that "by the works of the Law no flesh will be justified in His sight" (Rom. 3:20). God alone can cause such a man to see the true condition of his soul through the light of the gospel.

I remember a cold winter's day in Montana when I helped a friend retrieve some materials in a sealed-off cave where miners kept explosives. As we opened the steel door and entered, we could barely see due to the tiny flashlight my friend held in his hand. So he said, "Hang on, I'll go to the truck and get a bigger light." As he left, I shut the door to keep out the cold and stood there in darkness so black, it was as if I could feel it. Within a minute he returned with a brighter light, and, to our horror, we could suddenly see dozens of rattle snakes lying all around on the ground and on wooden crates of dynamite and boxes of tools. Some were easily within striking distance of where I stood in the dark, but the darkness had prevented me from seeing them. Fortunately, they were hibernating and the cold had slowed their metabolism, so they weren't a real danger. But that scene has stuck with me for many years. It perfectly illustrates man's need for the light of the gospel to show him the danger of those loathsome creatures of sin that he cannot see and that dwell in his heart. Such is the condition of fallen man. He simply cannot see what threatens to destroy him—*eternally*.

Knowing this, God must do what only He can do to show sinners the terrifying truth about their pathetic standing before His holy and righteous presence—a standing woefully insufficient to garner the verdict, "not guilty." The godly Reformed theologian Francis Turretin (1623-1687) described this awakening in a way that continues to grip my soul and make me forever thankful for the gift of spiritual sight:

> Hither our eyes must be altogether raised if we wish to inquire profitably concerning true righteousness; in what way we may answer the heavenly Judge, when he shall have called us to account. Truly while among men the comparison holds good; each one supposes he has what is of some worth and value. But when we rise to the heavenly tribunal and place before our eyes that supreme Judge . . .

by whose brightness the stars are darkened, at whose strength the mountains melt; by whose anger the earth is shaken; whose justice not even the angels are equal to bear; who does not make the guilty innocent; whose vengeance when once kindled penetrates even the lowest depths of hell . . . then in an instant the vain confidence of men perishes and falls and conscience is compelled . . . to confess that it has nothing upon which it can rely before God. And so it cries out with David, "Lord, if thou marked iniquity, who can stand?". . . When the mind is thoroughly terrified with the consciousness of sin and a sense of God's wrath, what is that thing on account of which he may be acquitted before God and be reckoned a righteous person? . . . Is it righteousness inhering in us and inchoate holiness or the righteousness and obedience of Christ alone imputed to us?[3]

The Spirit's work of regeneration that imparts spiritual life to the spiritually dead and causes a sinner to see his self-righteous pride and plead for undeserved mercy is a miracle that rivals creation itself. Like the tax collector who knew he was utterly devoid of any inherent righteousness — a man who "was even unwilling to lift up his eyes to heaven, but was beating his breast, saying, 'God, be merciful to me, the sinner'" (Luke 18:13)! And, with that act of repentant faith, he was instantly forgiven. Moreover, God's perfect righteousness was imputed to his account; he was justified by faith, ending the war of sin and gaining eternal peace with God through His grace alone. What a magnificent illustration of the doctrine of justification by faith—a divine treasure of unspeakable blessings that cannot be earned or forfeited.

Too often as believers I fear we are like the Black Skimmer who only skims the surface of the waters with his bill to catch his prey rather than diving deep into the ocean depths of divine truth, especially as it relates to our justification. It is easy to skim over the astonishing reality that it is through Christ "we have now received the reconciliation" (Rom. 5:11); and in Him there is treasured up all the fullness of wisdom and knowledge (Col. 2:3). It is the purpose of this mini-book to take us deeper into the ocean depths of divine revelation regarding this great doctrine, that together we might enjoy more fully the peace that is ours through justification, and cultivate a richer communion with the Lord Jesus Christ, the Lover of our soul.

In so doing we will discover how justification assures all believers that their salvation is eternally secured by the very One who saved them. While many passages refute the erroneous notion that a believer can forfeit (lose) his or her salvation—and in fact there is not a single text that, when properly interpreted, makes such a claim—the doctrine of justification brings an end to the argument.

Think about it: Paul writes, "Therefore having been justified by faith, we have . . ." The phrase "we have" indicates that what follows is already in our possession (Rom. 5:1), not something requiring ongoing merit. Sadly, many believers do not realize and can hardly imagine the present benefits of their justification, especially as it relates to assurance.

If you struggle with fear concerning your eternal security, then understanding the magnificent benefits of this marvelous doctrine will bring you the clarity and comfort you long for. Ongoing worry about salvation is really a needless concern for all who have been justified, because salvation is "a gift by His grace through the redemption which is in Christ Jesus" (Rom. 3:24), "an inheritance which is imperishable and undefiled and will not fade away, reserved in heaven for you, who are protected by the power of God through faith for a salvation ready to be revealed in the last time" (1 Peter 1:4-5).

Moreover, these profound truths speak to the very

core of who we are as believers and they have practical application for every aspect of Christian living.

Our First Present Benefit: Peace with God

Consider the first benefit. In Romans 5:1, Paul makes this startling declaration: "Therefore having been justified by faith, we have peace with God through our Lord Jesus Christ." There it is—the first benefit of our justification is *peace with God*. This refers to an *objective* peace, not merely a *subjective* peace. The war between a holy God and a sinful individual ends instantly and eternally the moment God makes His judicial declaration. Eternal reconciliation is secured the very instant we receive the divine gift whereby God imputes to us the righteousness of Christ—when He declares us righteous and forever treats us as such. Paul puts it this way in Romans 4:5: "But to the one who does not work, but believes in Him who justifies the ungodly, his faith is reckoned as righteousness." As a result, this *objective* peace will lead to a life-sustaining, soul-enriching, *subjective* peace as the internal experience of every saint, that "peace of God, which surpasses all comprehension, [that] shall guard [our] hearts and [our] minds in Christ Jesus" (Phil. 4:7).

The Believer's Union with Christ

To say we are justified is also to say that we are *united* to Christ. God no longer sees our sin—past, present and future. Instead, when He looks at us, He sees us clothed in the righteousness of Christ. This identification with Christ secures the redemption He accomplished on our behalf. Consider the multitude of Scripture texts on this theme: we have been "crucified with Christ" (Gal. 2:20); we have "died with Christ" (Col. 2:20); we have been "buried with Him" (Rom. 6:4); we have been "raised up together . . . in Christ" and "seated together in heavenly places in Christ" (Eph. 2:6); and our "life is hidden with Christ in God" (3:10).

That is not all! Our union with Christ secures our participation in all the spiritual blessings we have in Christ. There is "no condemnation for those who are in Christ" (Rom. 8:1); in Christ we are "free from the law of sin and death" (v. 2); we have "become the righteousness of God in Him" (2 Cor. 5:21); "in Christ" we have "wisdom, righteousness and sanctification, and redemption" (1 Cor. 1:30); and "if Christ is in you"... he "will also give life to your mortal bodies through His Spirit who indwells you" (Rom. 8:10, 11); "in Him [we] have been made complete" (Col. 2:10); and because of this glorious union, we are promised that "the dead in Christ shall rise first" (1 Thess. 4:16).

Within the pages of Scripture, the Holy Spirit describes this mysterious union through the use of various figures. In Romans 7:4, we are pictured as being *married to Christ*. In Ephesians 5, we are described as the *bride of the Groom*. In John 15, we see our union with Christ depicted as a *vine and branches*, showing the life-giving, organic bond we have with Him (we share the likeness of His nature, the infusing of eternal life, and the ability to bear spiritual fruit). In John 6, our union is pictured in the figure of *the body and food*; we have life by partaking of Christ, "the bread of life" (John 6:48), even as Christ had life by partaking of the Father (John 6:57). Paul depicts our union in the figure of Christ being *the Head and the church being His body* (Eph. 1:22-23). Paul also depicts the body of Christ as a *living organism*: "Now you are Christ's body, and individually members of it" (1 Cor. 12:27).

Because of our union with Christ, God does not look upon us with all our sin. Instead, He sees the righteousness of His beloved Son in whom we have been spiritually united. This is at the core of justification, and this is why we are at peace with God—forever.

Obviously, while we live out our lives in this human body, we continue to sin. Every honest believer acknowledges this, and certainly Scripture affirms it (1 John 1:8). Though we are no longer slaves to sin (Rom. 6:4), nevertheless we still sin. But the good news of the gospel is that Christ has paid our sins in full: "There is therefore now no condemnation for those who are in Christ Jesus" (Rom. 8:1; *cf.* Col. 1:19-22).

To put it another way, now that the battle is over, God is on our side. What do we have to be afraid of? "If God is for us, who is against us?" (Rom. 8:31). Talk about confident assurance! When we wear the armor God provides and our feet are "shod with the gospel of peace," we are able to "stand firm" (Eph. 6:11, 13). But, without this conviction, we will slip and slide and yield ground to the lies of the enemy. We will fall on our backs in doubt, discouragement, and confusion.

Sin also tends to trigger this, causing many believers to lack assurance because of guilt. In light of this, Peter exhorts every believer to be more diligent in his or her personal pursuit of holiness,

> applying all diligence, in your faith supply moral excellence . . . knowledge . . . self-control . . . perseverance . . . godliness . . . brotherly kindness, and in your brotherly kindness, love. For if these qualities are yours and are

increasing, they render you neither useless nor unfruitful in the true knowledge of our Lord Jesus Christ . . . . Therefore, brethren, *be all the more diligent to make certain about His calling and choosing you*; for as long as you practice these things, you will never stumble; for in this way the entrance into the eternal kingdom of our Lord and Savior Jesus Christ will be abundantly supplied to you (2 Peter 1: 5-11; emphasis mine).

When we understand that in our justification we have peace with God based solely upon what Christ has done as our substitute, then we grasp the reality that "He . . . was delivered over because of our transgressions, and was raised because of our justification" (Rom. 4:25). In Him we have a secure and sure footing. We are able to stand firm and stand our ground against the assaults of doubt. Only then can we share in Paul's confidence given to the saints at Philippi: "For I am confident of this very thing, that He who began a good work in you will perfect it until the day of Christ Jesus" (Phil. 1:6).

So, the first benefit of justification is that *God is at peace with us* and *we are now at peace with Him*. All that was lost at the Fall is now fully and eternally restored (though not fully experienced until heaven).

This peace also means we can be assured of our final destination. Because of the blood of the Lamb, and because we are forever united to Him, we have no reason to fear death or judgment.

Final Words

A person who is truly at peace with God is one who has first smelled the smoke of hell and knows that if it weren't for the mercy of God, that would be his eternal abode. He is a man so broken over his sin that he lives in perpetual wonder and awe because God has not only *forgiven* him, but He has imputed to him the very righteousness of Christ! God has literally declared him to be righteous, and now treats him as such! For this reason, every believer who treasures his justification will sing *Amazing Grace* as the doxology of his soul and will live in a constant state of breathless adoration of a God so merciful and compassionate.

Yes, a Christian will sin, but when he does, he will quickly repent. He will be broken and contrite over his sin and will not habitually live in the realm of its life-dominating power. Over time, he will experience an increasing hatred of sin and a decreasing frequency of it, and with Charles Wesley sing:

And can it be that I should gain
An interest in the Savior's blood?
Died he for me who caused His pain,
For me who Him to death pursued.
Amazing love, how can it be,
That Thou my God shouldst die for me?

Do not be deceived. If it is easy for you to knowingly and habitually rebel against God, then you will have no peace with Him, regardless of what you believe. The war is still on. You are not a sheep abiding in the fold of the great Shepherd. In John 10:27, Jesus said, "My sheep hear My voice and they know Me, and they follow Me." Or consider John's words in 1 John 2:3-5, "And by this we know that we have come to know Him, if we keep His commandments. The one who says, 'I have come to know Him,' and does not keep His commandments, is a liar, and the truth is not in him; but whoever keeps His word, in him the love of God has truly been perfected. By this we know that we are in Him."

While this magnificent doctrine is not a *license to sin*, it is a *deterrent from sin*. The celebration of our peace with God as our present and eternal possession will evoke the following doxology:

Despite my sin and stubborn pride
In love the Savior came.
Upon that dreadful cross He died
'Twas there He took my blame.

Oh what words could 'ere express
The marvels of His grace?
What love imputes Christ's righteousness
To such a rebel race?

But oh to grasp, the war is o'er!
God's wrath has been appeased!
Now justified, He sees no more
My rebellion and misdeeds.

Peace at last! Through Christ I come,
Through Him I stand in grace!
Before the glorious, holy throne,
Redeemed, to sing His praise.

What then, with so much mercy shown,
Should be my just reply?
To live by faith, each sin to mourn,
And serve my God Most High.

—D.A.H.

2

Access to God

> . . . *we have peace with God through our Lord Jesus Christ, through whom also we have obtained our introduction by faith.*
> ROMANS 5:1-2

As great as it is to have "peace with God" (Rom. 5:1), peace is only the beginning of the full benefits of justification that anchors our assurance in the divine promises of covenantal grace. In fact, it is our peace with God that allows us to experience the second benefit of our justification—*access to God*. The apostle Paul reveals this astonishing truth when he says that through our Lord Jesus Christ, "we have obtained our introduction by faith into this grace in which we stand" (Rom. 5:2).

Paul emphasizes that this reconciliation has happened to us *once and for all*. Remember, prior to our salvation, God was completely inaccessible and unapproachable. But at a certain point in time, access was granted. We were introduced into the royal chamber of our sovereign Monarch to pay Him homage, do His bidding, and enjoy sweet fellowship with Him. The phrase, "we have obtained our introduction" emphasizes that *this access is not something based upon the exercise of our will*. Furthermore, because the verb is in the perfect tense, we understand that our introduction to God has an ongoing effect as the result of a past action—Christ's redemptive work. Christ introduces us to the Father, through the cross.

This helps us also understand, contrary to the opinion of some, that justification is not a process involving our works. Rather, our justification is a divine declaration, a completely one-sided and eternal decree of our merciful God toward us through Christ. Because of Christ who makes our introduction, we are made acceptable to God and have assurance that He is favorably disposed to us, even welcoming us. Therefore, we have access into His holy presence. Inconceivable!

Paul elaborates on this in Ephesians 2:18 where he writes, "Through Him we both [referring to both Jews and Gentiles] have our access in one Spirit to the Father." Then, in Ephesians 3:12 he says, "In Him [that is, in Christ] we have boldness and confident access through faith in Him."

The Holiness of God

When we grasp the reality of the holiness of God, having access to Him becomes all the more astounding. Because God abhors sin, such a privilege is impossible and unfathomable. Throughout Scripture, God makes it clear that He dwells in a sacred realm, transcendent and unapproachable, set apart from the realm of mankind and unpolluted by sin. God loathes all things contrary to His Law. Holiness is His all-encompassing attribute. It portrays His consummate perfection and eternal glory. Like no other attribute God used to describe Himself in Scripture, Holiness stands alone as the defining characteristic of His person, the quintessential summation of all His attributes. He is the essence of purity, wholly without moral imperfection. His nature is the antithesis of the nature of man. Sin's corruption can be seen in man's innate inability to conform to the moral character and desires of God, a reality perfectly reflected in Solomon's ancient analysis of man's depraved condition where he says, "Furthermore, the hearts of the sons of men are full of evil, and insanity is in their hearts throughout their lives" (Eccl. 9:3).

Because of Adam's rebellion in the garden, the entire human race was plunged into sin (Rom. 5:12) and every child is conceived in a state of depravity. David put it this way: "Behold, I was brought forth in iniquity, and in sin my mother conceived me" (Ps. 51:5). Sin has penetrated and corrupted the whole of man's being (Isa. 1:6; Eph. 4:17-19), including his body (Rom. 8:10), his mind (Rom. 8:6; 1 Cor. 2:14; 4:4; Tit. 1:15); his will (John 8:34; Jer. 13:23; Rom. 7:18); and his heart (Jer. 17:9). Like a diamond contrasted against black velvet, the purity of divine holiness shines even more brilliantly against the blackness of man's sin.

But how can we, as finite and sinful creatures, possibly enter into His holy realm? The answer is found in the doctrine of justification. God made a way for us to be holy, even as He is holy, through the imputed righteousness of His beloved Son, the Lord Jesus Christ. For this reason, Jude bursts forth with a magnificent doxology: "Now to Him who is able to keep you from stumbling, and to make you stand in the presence of His glory blameless with great joy" (Jude 24).

The Heavenly Temple

To more fully appreciate the infinite chasm between God's holiness and man's sin, it is important to understand what God revealed to us about His sanctuary. There, God dwells separated from sin, a realm of perfect holiness: "For thus says the high and exalted One Who lives forever, whose name is Holy, 'I dwell on a high and holy place'" (Isa. 57:15; *cf.* 1 Kings 8:30; 2 Chron. 30:27; Ps. 123:1). This Heavenly Temple became the prototype God used to create His first sanctuary on earth, the Garden of Eden, and later the earthly tabernacle and temple (Ex. 25:8-9,40; *cf.* Ex. 26:30; 27:8; Num. 8:4; 1 Chron. 28:11-19).

Prior to sin, man enjoyed sweet fellowship with God in the Garden, the place where His presence on earth mirrored the court of God in heaven. Because of this, there is a definite connection between the Garden of Eden and the earthly sanctuaries God designed in the Tabernacle and Temple. This can be seen in how the geography and landscape of Eden corresponds to the physical arrangement and even the sacred objects of the Tabernacle and Temples.

Because of sin, however, "God drove the man out; and at the east of the garden of Eden He stationed the cherubim and the flaming sword which turned every direction to guard the way to the tree of life"

(Gen. 3:24). This corresponds with two cherubim that guarded the Mercy Seat on the Ark of the Covenant in the Tabernacle and the Temple, the only place where God would meet with man (Ex. 25:18-22; 26:1,31; 1 Kings 8:4-7). The terrifying presence of the cherubim with their flaming swords speaks strongly about God's intention to judge any sinful man who would dare approach His holy presence.

Although man could no longer return to God because of sin, God in His infinite mercy was willing to return to man—not physically, but *spiritually*. On Mt. Sinai, God revealed His Law to Moses and instituted the Tabernacle that would replace the Garden Sanctuary (Ex. 19-40:38). And in the innermost sanctuary of that structure, God provided a way for sinners to enter into His holy presence through a mediated entrance made possible by the priesthood He established (Lev. 1-7). While the cherubim in Eden faced *outward* to prevent sinful man from returning to the presence of God in his defiled condition, those stationed above the Mercy Seat faced *inward* to invite sinful man into His presence on the basis of the blood of an innocent sacrifice sprinkled on the Mercy Seat on the Day of Atonement. All of this pointed to our perfect High Priest, the spotless Lamb of God, the Lord Jesus Christ, who satisfied the justice of God for the sins of all who would place their trust in Him.

The Boundaries of the Earthly Tabernacle and Temples

The same kinds of boundaries God placed at the Garden after sin were also put in place in the Tabernacle and in the Temple. The first mention of the Temple in Scripture is in Exodus 15:17, where, after the successful crossing of the Red Sea, Moses breaks forth in praise and declares, "You, Lord, will bring them and plant them in the mountain of Your inheritance, the place, O Lord, which You have made for Your dwelling, the sanctuary, O Lord, which Your hands have established."

That God was unapproachable due to His holiness can be seen in His layout of the Temple. First, there was an outer court for the Gentiles. Then, a little further in, there was another court for Jewish women. Then, further still was another court for the Jewish men and the priests. In fact, if you look at the current Wailing Wall in Jerusalem today, you will see the men gathered at the base and the women over on the side. This segregation is intended to honor God's original plan.

Morally speaking, anything that is "holy" is set apart or separated from sin and consecrated to God. For this reason the Old Testament speaks frequently about maintaining the distinction between things that are sacred and those considered secular or worldly. We see this pictured in the Tabernacle where every aspect of that ancient place of worship symbolized the priority of being separate from the world. In the innermost part of the Tabernacle, God erected the most holy place that housed the Ark of the Covenant. He commanded that it be devoted solely to His service and separated from the sinfulness of the world by a veil (Ex. 26:33).

Inside the Ark was the Holy Standard, the Law of Moses given on Mt. Sinai. Above the Ark on each end were golden cherubs with outstretched wings symbolically guarding the holiness of God. Between the cherubs hovered the *shekinah* glory of God, the light of His presence, too brilliant to be seen by the fallen eyes of man. On top of the Ark was a golden lid that separated the Law within from the Holy presence above, thus symbolizing that the Law had been violated and God's holiness cannot be contaminated by sin.

All of this had profound implications for sinful humanity in need of being reconciled to a holy God, for it was upon this lid that divine justice and grace came together symbolically. Once a year on the Day of Atonement, the holiest of days, the High Priest sprinkled the blood of an animal on that golden lid of separation. That lid was called the "Mercy Seat," the *hilasterion* in the Septuagint (the Greek translation of the Old Testament). This word means "to appease, to placate, or to satisfy." This was the sacrifice of atonement. The same term was used in 1 John 2:1 to describe "Jesus Christ the righteous; and He Himself is the propitiation (*hilasmos*) for our sins." Likewise we read in 1 John 4:

> ...God has sent His only begotten Son into the world so that we might live through Him. In this is love, not that we loved God, but that He loved us and sent His Son to be the propitiation [hilasmos] for our sins (vv. 9b, 10).

The amazing truth of the gospel of Christ was thereby foreshadowed in the sacrificial system. The Lord clarified this when He stated in Exodus 25:21,22:

> You shall put the mercy seat [hilasterion] on top of the ark, and in the ark you shall put the testimony which I will give to you. There I will meet with you; and from above the mercy seat, from between the two cherubim which are upon the ark of the testimony.

The Mercy Seat was the place where the righteous wrath of God was symbolically propitiated and where divine fury was temporarily appeased. Only the most hardened sinner or superficial Christian could possibly contemplate such a scene and yet remain indifferent to the transcendent holiness of God, His hatred of sin, and His mercy and grace offered to sinners through Jesus Christ. For He was the One who "entered the Most Holy Place once for all, having obtained eternal redemption" (Heb. 9:12). *Jesus is our propitiation.*

All of this pointed to the blood of Christ that would once and for all make atonement for the sins of all who place their trust in Him. His sacrifice gives us access into the presence of a holy God. The purpose of the penal substitution and the sacrificial system ("penal" referring to the severe punishment of the substitute) was to graphically illustrate the punishment of sin and to demand that the people have an inward identification with that sin. The purpose of the final sacrifice of Christ was to pay for all the sin to which all those sacrifices pointed.

Those Old Testament sacrifices were effective, but they were not *expiatory*—they could not remove guilt or sin. Though they were effective for temporary, ritual restoration (the cleansing of the flesh according to Hebrews 9:13), they could not permanently remove the guilt of sin. Such a permanent remedy would require a totally innocent human substitute, someone who had perfectly obeyed the Law and was in every way perfect and pure, and therefore was able to die in the place of sinners.

Of course, that could only be the Lord Jesus. He was the only possible substitute. He offered Himself in our place to both *expiate*, (remove the guilt of our sin) and *propitiate* (appease the righteous wrath of God against sin). Recall what happened when Jesus died on the cross. At the very moment His life ended, something almost incredible happened at the entrance to the Holy of Holies. According to Matthew 27:51, the veil of the Temple was torn in two, from top to bottom—solely by the power of God. Can there be a more dramatic demonstration of our access into the presence of God? We no longer need an ordinary priest to go into God's presence on our behalf, because we have our introduction through the Lord Jesus, our faithful High Priest. His death removed the barrier of sin.

Expiation, Propitiation, and Justification

But, how did Jesus' death enable us to gain access to God? The answer is simple, yet profound: the blood of Christ removed the guilt of our sin (*expiation*) and His blood appeased the righteous wrath of God against sin (*propitiation*). The moment we are born again, God imputes the righteousness of Christ to all who believe in Him, declaring them forgiven and treating them as totally righteous forever (*justification*). Thus, "we have obtained our introduction by faith" (Rom. 5:2). In light of this truth, the writer of Hebrews says:

> Since therefore, brethren, we have confidence to enter the holy place by the blood of Jesus, by a new and living way which He inaugurated for us through the veil, that is, His flesh, and since we have a great priest over the house of God, let us draw near with a sincere heart in full assurance of faith, having our hearts sprinkled clean from an evil conscience and our bodies washed with pure water (Heb. 10:19-22).

As glorious as it is to know that we not only have *peace with God* and eternal *access into His presence*, these only represent the necessary foundation upon which an incomprehensibly glorious superstructure must rest—the edifice of Christ's bridal church. We now consider the third benefit of our justification as we see this mysterious and marvelous structure begin to form in our mind's eye.

3

A Permanent Standing Before God

> . . . *we have obtained our introduction by faith into this grace in which we stand.*
> ROMANS 5:3

It always amazes me to see the Holy Spirit use His Word to raise the spiritually dead to newness of life and transform thoughts of hopeless despair into exhilarating joy. If you belong to the company of the redeemed, you have no reason to fear, because you are a child of the King.

It is no wonder the apostle Paul was filled with joy and gratitude despite all the problems he endured. He viewed life through the lens of the astounding benefits of justification.

By way of review, the first benefit we learned

about is that we have peace with God (Rom. 5:1). The second benefit is that *we have access to God* (Rom. 5:2). Because Christ permanently removed the guilt of our sin and appeased the righteous wrath of God against sin, we can enter into His holy presence (Heb. 10:19-22). As a result of these first two benefits we now have *a permanent standing before God*.

In Romans 5:2 we read that because of Christ, "we have obtained our introduction by faith into this grace in which we stand." If you struggle with the assurance of your salvation, then you can put that forever behind you because of this text alone. This is the very purpose for which it was written.

The word "stand" comes from a Greek term meaning "to stand fast." It means that *something is established or fixed in a place so as never to be moved*. And, what is this place? It is the *position of grace*. Psalm 130:3-4 says, "If You, Lord, should mark iniquities, O Lord, who could stand?" The answer is, *no one*. But he goes on to say, "But there is forgiveness with You."

When the fury of God's wrath upon the world is poured out just prior to Christ's glorious return, the ungodly will cry out for the mountains and the rocks to hide them from the wrath of the Lamb. They will say, "For the great day of their wrath has come; and who is able to stand" (Rev. 6:16-17)? Who might that be? *Only those who have been justified and therefore stand in grace.*

Because we are *in Christ*, we stand safe and secure before God. There is no condemnation for those who are in Him (Rom. 8:1). Moreover, we do not look to ourselves to maintain this position of grace, because we have no righteousness of our own. Instead, the believer *obtains* his introduction by faith in Christ, and because of this divine gift, he enters into a permanent state of justification whereby he is able to receive all the blessings of the condition he now enjoys.

In Romans 6, Paul explains that before we were justified, in our unsaved condition we were under the law and therefore in a state of condemnation and slavery to sin. But now, because of this new standing in grace, we have been freed—not free to sin, but free *not* to sin. Therefore, he says, "For sin shall not be master over you"(Rom. 6:14). Why? Paul answers: "For you are not under law, but under grace."

This reality animates Jude's doxology when he speaks of our Lord Jesus Christ as the one "who is able to keep you from stumbling" (Jude 24). The word "keep" carries the idea of *keeping something secure in the midst of an attack.* The Lord Jesus does this work, and for this reason, Jude goes on to say He will "make you stand in the presence of His glory blameless with great joy."

Contrast this with the unsaved who are still under the law; they "will not stand in the judgment" (Ps. 1:5). They will be without defense, unable to stand their ground. Further, there will be no "sinners in the assembly of the righteous" (v. 5) because they are still at war with God. They have no access to God, nor do they have a permanent standing in grace. Only those who have *obtained their introduction by faith into this grace in which we stand* will ever be in the presence of God and in the assembly of the righteous.

This is our permanent standing before God. It is firmly fixed forever. Stated differently, there is nothing transient about this state. There is nothing tenuous or fragile about this position. Nothing about this status will require us to up the ante of our obedience in order for it to remain.

The Power of Being Convinced

In light of this standing in grace before God, Paul later declares, "I am convinced" (Rom. 8:38). *Convinced*—I love that word, don't you? Because we stand in grace, Paul is convinced:

that neither death, nor life, nor angels, nor principalities, nor things present, nor things to come, nor powers, nor height, nor depth, nor any other created thing, shall be able to separate us from the love of God, which is in Christ Jesus our Lord (Rom. 8:38).

Likewise, in order for the Corinthian Christians to truly be able to enjoy this established position, the apostle Paul declares, "Now I make known to you, brethren, the gospel which I preached to you, which also you received, in which also you stand, by which also you are saved"(1 Cor. 15:1-2). The grammar Paul uses here is very important. The term "saved" means that *you are continually rescued by someone other than yourself.* This means believers make no contribution to their salvation. It is all of grace!

That text goes on to say, ". . . if you hold fast the word which I preached to you"(1 Cor. 15:2). This was a warning to those phony professors who had a non-saving faith, who believed the gospel to be true, but had never genuinely repented of their sins and embraced Christ as Savior. The verse could be rendered, "If you hold fast or give evidence to what I preached to you, unless your faith is worthless or unless you believed without effect." Bottom line, those who stand in grace *will* hold fast. They *will* persevere in the faith.

Those Who Have Fallen from Grace

Now, some readers might ask, "What about Galatians 5:4, which says, 'You have been severed from Christ, you who are seeking to be justified by law; you have fallen from grace.' Doesn't Paul argue that a man can be severed from Christ and fall from grace?"

Such an interpretation disregards the context and is therefore erroneous. Moreover, if that were true, many passages that say quite the opposite would all be called into question, for God does not contradict Himself.

In Galatians 5, Paul is not speaking about the security of the believer. He's not even speaking to believers. He's addressing the legalistic Jew who seeks to be justified by keeping the law rather than by grace through faith. He's arguing that law and grace do not mix—they are mutually exclusive. The man who comes to Christ for salvation by grace, but then tries to supplement grace through acts of legalism under the law, severs himself from Christ. "Severed" means separated, loosed, or estranged. Thus, "You are seeking to be justified by law. You have fallen from grace."

The term "fallen" used here means to lose one's grasp on something, or to be driven off course. Such a man is not here being described as one who is *un*justified—as though God reverses His previous adjudication and rescinds His former declaration. The Bible knows nothing of that. The self-righteous law-keeper has not lost his standing in grace, because he never had it in the first place. He has been severed from Christ in that his legalism is antithetical to reliance upon Christ's saving grace as being sufficient to save him and to keep him safe. Therefore, because he thinks Christ's righteousness is insufficient and he must add his works of the law to be saved, he has indeed, fallen from grace. He has lost his grasp of the principle of saving grace. But that is not to say he has lost his salvation, because a man cannot lose what he never possessed.

Those Who Have Fallen Away

Hebrews 6:6 also causes concern for many, with its description of people who "have fallen away." Again, understanding the idea in its context is crucial. In Hebrews 6, the author addressed unbelieving Jews who, according to the first two verses, were still seeking to be justified by works of the law. They had once been enlightened and informed, having tasted of the heavenly gift (Heb. 6:4). The word "tasted" means *sampled*. They tried the flavor of the gospel, but never swallowed it to be saved. They pondered the truths of the gospel of grace and even experienced some of the temporary blessings of Christ's miracles in their midst. For instance, by the time of the end of Christ's ministry, there was hardly any disease in Palestine. Many witnessed this personally. But they never wholeheartedly embraced Jesus as their Messiah and Savior from sin.

This idea of "taste" is also used in speaking of Christ tasting death (Heb. 2:9), referring to something that is *fleeting* and *temporary—not permanent*. These unsaved Jews had a temporary, fleeting taste of the blessings of Christ. They saw His miracles, and maybe even experienced them. They saw the healing of the sick, the casting out of demons, and the feeding of the hungry.

Hebrews goes on to say that they have "tasted of the heavenly gift and have been made partakers of the Holy Spirit"(Heb. 6:4). "Partakers" here speaks of *association*, not of *possession*. Luke uses the word to describe fishing partners who were in *association* with one another (Luke 5:7). Hebrews 1:9 uses the same word to refer to the angels being in *association* with Christ as His companions. So the point is, these Jews were in *association* with the Holy Spirit, but they did not *possess* Him.

They witnessed the Spirit-empowered miracles of Jesus, but the Holy Spirit did not inhabit them because they were not saved. Many had experienced His convicting work even in their lives, but they refused to believe. They "tasted the good word of God and the powers of the age to come" (Heb. 6:5). Again, this is not speaking of salvation. The word "word" (*rhema*) here refers to that which has been uttered by a living voice and it emphasizes the *parts* of the word rather than the *whole*. If he was referring to the whole word, he would have used the Greek word that makes that distinction (*logos*), but he does not. So they have tasted only a part of the word. They have only heard elements of the gospel.

Continuing on, the writer states, "...and then have fallen away" (Heb. 6:6). But, *from what have they fallen away*? Not from salvation. There is no indication they ever possessed saving faith, so it would be impossible to fall from a place where they had never stood. In fact, the whole context tells us that they rejected it, preferring salvation by works instead. So, *they have fallen away from the knowledge of the truth*. They heard the truth, but they refused it. Instead they said, "No, I don't want that. I believe a man is justified by works, not by grace alone through faith alone."

So indeed, they fell away from the principles of justification. The word for "falling away" in the original Greek means *to slip aside* or *to deviate from the right path*. Context helps us understand that they deviated from the one true path that leads to salvation. This is the sin of unbelief, a sin so severe that the writer goes on to say, "It is impossible to renew them again to repentance, since they again crucify to themselves the Son of God, and put Him to open shame" (Heb. 6:6). In other words, by rejecting His gift of grace, they treated the Lord Jesus as if He deserved to be crucified—as if to say, "If you insist in rejecting Him, especially in light of full revelation of the truth, then you have no hope for salvation because there is no other way to be saved!"

So, this section in Hebrews 6 gives warning to *unbelievers*. This becomes obvious when contrasted to the next section, in which the author makes a shift to speak to *believers*. He says, "But, *beloved*, we are convinced of better things concerning you" (Heb. 6:9; emphasis mine). We must be careful not to allow a misinterpretation of Scripture to undermine the foundation of our faith and our standing in grace. Don't be deceived into thinking that we can fall away from what God has eternally decreed in sovereign election and granted in salvation. True believers permanently stand in grace (*cf.* 1 Peter 1:3-5).

Those Who Apostatize

"But wait a minute," some might say, "What about those believers who apostatize? What about those who walk with Christ for years and then renounce the faith? Explain that."

The Scripture is very clear about those people; *they were never truly saved*. They were like Judas who knew and served Jesus, and even fooled his closest companions, yet betrayed Christ and perished in his sins. Those who apostatize were not standing in grace. Theirs was a dead faith. They were tares amongst the wheat. They looked like the real thing, but they weren't. As 1 John 2:19 makes clear, "They went out from us, but they were not really of us; for if they had been of us, they would have remained with us; but they went out, in order that it might be shown that they all are not of us." Also, in 1 John 3:9 and 10 we read, "No one who is born of God practices sin. . . . Anyone who does not practice righteousness is not of God." Life-dominating sin committed with impunity and apostasy are incompatible with the ministry of the Holy Spirit who has imparted a new nature to every true believer (John 3:5-8; *cf.* 2 Cor. 5:17). Such an anti-Christ spirit describes "everyone whose name has not been written from the foundation of the world in the book of life of the Lamb who has been slain" (Rev. 13:8).

Maintain the Big Picture of Redemption

It is also crucial that we not lose sight of God's predetermined plan of redemption. Go back to the big picture. Remember that in eternity past the Father ordained a plan to demonstrate His infinite love for His Son whereby He chose for Him a bride. And that bride is made up of undeserving sinners whom He would one day justify by His grace. He chose them by name. He recorded their names in a book of life. These would be the names that would make up the Son's bride, an elect group of redeemed humanity pledged to Him as a gift of the Father's love, a pledge that was sealed by the Holy Spirit.

Central to this whole predetermined plan of inner-Trinitarian love and glory was the Son's death. So, the Lord Jesus came to do the will of the Father—to fully and eternally save all that the Father had given Him. Jesus became the perfect substitute for sinners in order for them to be reconciled to a holy God.

When, by grace through faith, the Holy Spirit regenerates a sinner and causes him to believe, not only is he forgiven that very moment, but the righteousness of Christ is also imputed to him. He is eternally *justified*. He suddenly has *peace with God, access to God* and he forever *stands in grace*. He never falls away because it is all a work of God. He is established in that state forever by divine grace. Jesus said, "I give eternal life to [those who are His], and they shall never perish; and no one shall snatch them out of My hand" (John 10:28).

Given these assuring truths, Paul prayed: "Now may the God of peace Himself sanctify you entirely; and may your spirit and soul and body be preserved complete, without blame at the coming of our Lord Jesus Christ. Faithful is He who calls you, and He also will bring it to pass" (1 Thess. 5:23-4). May this express your confidence as well.

Having examined our *peace with God*, our *access to God*, and our *permanent standing before God*, we now turn to the fourth blessing of our justification: *our jubilant hope of glory*.

4

A Jubilant Hope of Glory

> *. . . and we exult in hope of the glory of God.*
> ROMANS 5:2

Jesus says, "I came that they might have life, and might have it abundantly" (John 10:10), and John writes, "God has given us eternal life, and this life is in His Son. He who has the Son has the life; he who does not have the Son of God does not have the life" (1 John 5:11). What a marvelous promise! And to think that for all who have been united to Christ by faith, *this abundant life begins now,* because at the moment of the new birth, the righteousness of Christ is imputed to us. We are declared to be righteous. We are acceptable to God and He takes up permanent residence in us. As a result of this supernatural transaction, every believer can instantly begin to enjoy the rich blessings of justification.

We have already examined the first three: *peace with God, access to God*, and *a permanent standing before God*. Now, we come to the fourth magnificent benefit of justification: *a jubilant hope of glory*.

Regaining the Glory Lost

Previously Paul reminded us that "all have sinned and fall short of the glory of God" (Romans 3:23). Grammatically, this phrase is in the present tense, meaning all are *continuously* falling short. Moreover, the way the verb is constructed (the middle voice in Greek) indicates that the cause of our dreadful condition of sin is not something outside of us, but *from within*. It's because of our own sin nature that we are continuously falling short of God's glory. Our lives were meant to reflect His majesty and redound to His glory. But thankfully, justification made possible what our sin nature prevented.

Notice again the same phrase in verse two. Because we are at peace with God, because we have access to God, and because we have a permanent standing in grace, "We exult in hope of the glory of God"(Romans 5:2). The word "exult" in the original language can be translated, "to rejoice, to revel, to boast, to glory on account of a thing." And in this context we could paraphrase it this way: "You need to jump for joy in sheer jubilation when you reflect upon your immovable standing in grace that is the basis of your confident hope of future bliss." To be sure, we have a divinely granted and guarded salvation that anchors our hope of one day sharing in the glory of God.

When we examine the phrase, "We exult in hope of the glory of God" (Rom. 5:2), we see there are two events that await us, events every justified saint will someday experience. First, *we are going to experience an unrestricted, personal fellowship with the Triune God*. Second, *we are going to experience a personal transformation into the glory of Christ*. This is why we exult in hope of the glory of God. The reality of these discoveries should animate our heart to praise and greatly impact how we live. It certainly governed the life of the apostle Paul.

1. Unrestricted Personal Fellowship with God

First, let's examine this idea of having an *unrestricted personal fellowship with the Triune God*. Can you imagine what it will be like when we see God face-to-face? Yet this will be one of the blessings that belong to the redeemed. Jesus promised, "Blessed are the pure in heart, for they shall see God" (Matt 5:8).

But, how can we have purity of heart since we already know that it doesn't come from anything we can do? The answer is found in the theme of Paul's argument: *purity in heart is the result of justification*. Only the justified will be able to experience unrestricted, personal fellowship with the Triune God.

Paul writes, "For now we see in a mirror dimly, but then face to face; now I know in part, but then I shall know fully just as I also have been fully known" (1 Cor. 13:12). The Greek word "know" in this text means to accurately and intimately perceive and understand. Not only will we see the glory of God when we see Him face-to-face, but we will have the same kind of intimate understanding of His person and His character, likened to the knowledge that He has of us. Paul expresses this when he says, ". . . then I shall know fully just as I also have been fully known" (1 Cor. 13:12).

Staggering, isn't it? Thrilling; motivating! No wonder Paul says, "I want you to rejoice in hope of the glory of God." He's saying, "I want you to be consumed with sheer jubilation when you reflect upon the immovable standing that is yours in grace that guarantees all of this will one day come to fruition when faith will be turned to sight." Therefore,

"Exult in hope of the glory of God" (Rom. 5:2).

Bear in mind that Paul had already experienced some measure of this when he penned these words to the saints in Rome. He knew exactly what awaited them. In fact, he gave us a glimpse of this intimate fellowship when he described to the Corinthians his own supernatural experience:

> I know a man in Christ who fourteen years ago—whether in the body I do not know, or out of the body I do not know, God knows—such a man was caught up to the third heaven. And I know how such a man—whether in the body or apart from the body I do not know, God knows—was caught up into Paradise, and heard inexpressible words, which a man is not permitted to speak (2 Cor. 12:2-4).

When we look at other writings of Paul we get some sense of what he saw and experienced. These things were so unspeakably glorious that all he could say was simply *exult in hope of the glory of God!* It's as though he smiles while shaking his head in dismay and says, "I can't even begin to describe this to you, but trust me: the glory of God exceeds the limits of anything you can imagine!"

In 2 Corinthians 12:5, Paul says something else that is very interesting about his encounter with God. He says, "On behalf of such a man will I boast; but on my own behalf I will not boast, except in regard to my weaknesses." The Greek word for "boast" is the same term used in Romans 5:2 where he says we "exult ("boast" or "rejoice") in hope of the glory of God". Paul is essentially saying, "I jump for joy in sheer jubilation when I reflect upon my confident hope of our future bliss—that which I saw and heard." This should be the response of every saint. Like Paul, we also "exult in the hope of the glory of God" because one day we will experience unrestricted personal fellowship with the Triune, thrice-holy God of the Bible!

One day we will see something so astounding, so breathtakingly transcendent, that, by comparison, "the sufferings of this present time are not worthy to be compared with the glory that is to be revealed to us" (Rom. 8:18). This will not only include the astounding splendors of heaven; but most importantly, it will comprehend an unrestricted personal fellowship with the Lover of our soul. We will be able to know God in ways exceedingly beyond our awareness of Him now.

2. A Personal Transformation into the Glory of Christ

Paul desires for us to be consumed with the exhilarating benefits of our justification. When we do, we inevitably exult in hope of the glory of God. This will not only include an *unrestricted personal fellowship with the triune God*, but, secondly, *a personal transformation into the glory of Christ*.

Consider two texts of Scripture. First, in Hebrews 1:3, the writer speaks of Jesus as being, "the radiance of [God's] glory and the exact representation of His nature." And Paul says, "For whom He foreknew, He also predestined to become conformed to the image of His Son" (Rom. 8:29). Putting these Scriptures together, we see that God has predestined believers to share in the likeness of God in terms of the glory of His character (*cf.* 1 Cor. 15:50, 53). Although we will have a different makeup with respect to how we are constructed, our external appearance will be like His.

The Father is not going to present to His Son an ugly bride. Instead, as we read in Ephesians 5:27, God desires to "present to Himself the church in all her glory, having no spot or wrinkle or any such thing; but that she should be holy and blameless." In fact, we have been "prepared beforehand for glory" (Rom. 9:23).

In 2 Corinthians 3:18, Paul adds this fascinating statement, "But we all being transformed into the same image from glory to glory, just as from the Lord, the Spirit." Think about this. Wherever you are right now, even as you are reading this mini-book, at this very moment you are *being transformed*. Grammatically, the phrase "being transformed" translates a present passive participle. It is from the verb *metamorphoo*, from which we get our word "metamorphosis." Notice, too, that this transformation happens in stages. We continue to do this as we behold Him—a continual and progressive process. Our sanctification is empowered by the indwelling Spirit of God, who alone can gradually conform us into the image of the Lord Jesus Christ.

This "being transformed" is similar to what Paul says in Romans 12:2, where he uses the same verb. There is a metamorphosis that occurs by the renewing of our mind. That is why Paul says that we are ascending from "glory to glory" until one day we are like Him (2 Cor. 3:18). As we see God and as we see the glory of Christ through Scripture, we gradually begin to manifest on the outside who we truly are on the inside.

Paul described it this way:

> For our citizenship is in heaven, from which also we eagerly wait for a Savior, the Lord Jesus Christ; who will transform the body of our humble state into conformity with the body of His glory, by the exertion of the power that He has even to subject all things to Himself (Phil. 3:20-21).

This subjection will undoubtedly include the creation of new laws of physics. Don't you long for that resurrected body? Oh, to be like Christ! As we study this in Scripture, it is more than simply a "new and improved" version of ourselves. No, it is a *totally new and completely recreated body*. In 1 Corinthians 15 Paul tells how we are going to be raised imperishable, in power. In death, what is sown in dishonor and weakness will be raised in glory and power. Like His own glorious body, we will be given a spiritual body beyond anything we can comprehend—one suited for eternal life beyond the limits of time and space in which we exist today.

The Motivating Force of Anticipated Glory

In 2 Corinthians 4:17-18, Paul anticipates this coming glory and his words help us to put our present sufferings into perspective. He says, "For momentary, light affliction is producing for us an eternal weight of glory far beyond all comparison." In short, future glory outweighs anything that we can experience in terms of suffering in this life. He goes on to say, "while we look not at the things which are seen, but at the things which are not seen; for the things which are seen are temporal, but the things which are not seen are eternal."

This should change our perspective. True endurance in the faith and overcoming the many obstacles we encounter in this fallen world requires looking beyond the temporal and the physical. Instead, we must gaze into the eternal through eyes of faith. Admittedly, we don't see completely or clearly right now, but we have a certain hope that one day we will see and experience all that He has granted us in the fullness of divinely wrought perfection.

And what is the basis of these promises in which we hope? It is our justification. Because we have been declared righteous, we have *access to God*; we have *peace with God*; we have *a permanent standing in grace*. Therefore Paul says, "Exult in hope of the glory of God"(Rom. 5:2).

It is not uncommon to experience the joys of Eden one minute and the sorrows of Gethsemane the next. But ultimately, because of our justification, we have the certain hope of seeing Christ in all His glory: "We know that when He appears, we will be like Him, because we will see Him just as He is" (1 John 3:2). Theologians have described this as the *Beatific Vision*—that moment when we will feast our souls on the visible presence of Christ and enjoy the infinite beauty and love of God forever. That day when we will see God and stand in His presence blameless with great joy" (Jude 24). That instant when, for the first time, we will experience the unhindered, perfected, fullness of Triune love. Can there be any greater promise to bring joy to our soul?

Oh, that we would rejoice in this blessed hope! There is a process of sanctification presently at work that will culminate in these glorious truths. That is why we can sing with Charles Wesley:

> *Changed from glory into glory,*
> *'Til in heaven we take our place,*
> *'Til we cast our crowns before thee,*
> *Lost in wonder, love and praise.*

And with this blessing resonating within our hearts, we can understand the fifth ascending benefit that rises from the glory of our justification: *joy in tribulation*.

5

Joy in Tribulation

And not only this, but we also exult in our tribulations.
ROMANS 5:3

As defined earlier, to be "justified" means to be declared righteous by a holy God—to have received the righteousness of Christ and therefore to be treated as such. As a result of this supernatural declaration, every believer may instantly begin to enjoy the unfathomable benefits of justification.

In our study of Romans 5:1-11, we have examined the first four of nine benefits of this God-given justification: peace with God, access to God, a permanent standing before God and a jubilant hope of glory. Now we will consider the fifth benefit of our justification: *joy in tribulation*, described in Romans 5:3: "And not only this, but we also exult in our tribulations, knowing that tribulation brings about perseverance."

The Triumph of Faith

Previously, we looked at the word "exult" in our study of Romans 5:2. There, it says, "We rejoice in hope of the glory of God." Whether translated "rejoice" or "exult," it is the same Greek word. It means to rejoice, to revel, or it can even mean to boast or glory on account of something—*in hope of our future glory*. But here in verse three he adds something else that is most remarkable. He says that because of our justification, *we can also rejoice in our present tribulations.* Our faith triumphs over tribulation because of the righteousness of Christ that we now possess!

"Tribulation" translates a Greek term that means a pressing or a squeezing together. It is used to describe the pressure that was exerted upon grapes or olives to be able to extract the precious juice or oil from them. And so this term "tribulation" refers to anguish of soul, and to affliction. Whenever we experience some distressing trial in our life, we know the agonizing pressure, the weight, and the stress it causes. It squeezes the very life out of us, especially when we are persecuted for our faith.

Tribulation is a very important topic, and it occupies a great amount of text in the New Testament. Jesus dealt with it head-on in the close of His earthly ministry. In John 16, He promised that the Helper would come—the Holy Spirit—who would dwell within every believer. He spoke of the power of prayer and how the Father would answer prayer on the basis of the merit of Christ and His righteousness. Then He warned, "I have said these things to you, that in me you may have peace. In the world you will have tribulation. But take heart; I have overcome the world" (John 16:33; *cf.* Acts 14:22). The only possible way we can endure tribulation with joy is through the persevering power brought about through our union with Christ.

The Power in Knowing God Is Up to Something

First, notice carefully the language the Holy Spirit uses here at the end of verse three: "We also exult in our tribulations" (Rom. 5:3). He is not saying we rejoice merely *in spite* of our tribulations, as if we merely resign ourselves to them and choose to be happy. Nor is he saying that we rejoice *in the midst* of our tribulations—though that is true. No, it is far more than that. His point is that we exult *because of* our tribulations, on account of them. This paints the canvas of our sufferings with bright colors of hope and portrays them with vivid importance. But why would we exult *on account* of the ruthless persecution of a world that hates Christ and all who belong to Him? The answer: *because God has ordained our tribulations for our good and for His glory.*

This is at the heart of Paul's fascinating statement in Philippians 1:29: "For to you it has been granted for Christ's sake, not only to believe in Him, but also to suffer for His sake." The word "granted" is a Greek verb that comes from the noun for *grace*. So it is as if he is saying here, "This is a gracious gift that God has given you to suffer for His sake." How can this possibly be? How can suffering be for our good? What gracious gift does God grant to us in the context of our tribulations?

Two very important words in verse three contain the answer. First, notice that Paul says, "we also exult in our tribulations, knowing . . ."(Rom. 5:3). The term "knowing" (in the original language) means to behold, perceive, discern, or to discover something. So, this joy in tribulation is a result of our *knowledge*. But, what must we know?

The Spirit of God answers this in verse three: "We also exult in our tribulations, knowing that tribulation brings about perseverance." The phrase "brings about" (in the original language) means to perform or accomplish something. God is performing something in our life through the means of a tribulation or trial. He is working something in us and that something is *perseverance, patience,* and *endurance*. All of this speaks of the character of a genuine believer. This is how a true child of God responds to tribulation. We must know that God is up to something in our life, that He is bringing about and teaching us perseverance, patience, and endurance.

God loves the justified sinner so much that He not only purchased our redemption with His very blood, but He intimately involves Himself in our life that He might work something in us, namely, *Christlikeness*. God uses tribulations and suffering to accomplish this purpose that our lives might display the love and loveliness of Christ to the praise of His glory.

Perhaps you can look back on some great trial you have survived and say, "Oh, my, what a work God did because of all of that! God brought about those tribulations to produce perseverance and steadfastness in me, that in all things Christ might have the preeminence!" To be sure, He is producing in us a faith that cannot be shaken—a steadfast faith that gives testimony to the power of Christ to save and sanctify. He strengthens us and produces in us a loyalty for Christ. When confronted with some great affliction, we see our faith and our piety actually increase rather than decrease. Paul is saying that the child of God who knows these things will be the one who rejoices in tribulation.

Ask, "What?" Not "Why?"

When we experience some severe trial in our life, we should never ask *why?* because God does not owe us an explanation, nor could we understand it if He offered one. Instead we should humbly ask, *what?* We should pray, "Father, I know You have ordained my affliction and somehow You are working something in me (and in other people) in ways I am unaware. Therefore, what would You have me do to give You glory in the midst of this trial? I know my sufferings will ultimately work together for my good and Your glory, so please help me understand through Your Word how I should respond."

Isn't it amazing how great trials drive us to our Rock and Refuge? When things are going well, we become overconfident, like Peter, who assured Jesus that he would never forsake Him. We get cocky. We get a little careless, and self-sufficient. But "Pride comes before a fall," doesn't it? How quickly we can lose sight of how utterly dependent we are upon our Lord who said, "Apart from Me, you can do nothing" (John 15:5).

Then, the phone rings. It's bad news—*really bad news*! And suddenly our life is changed forever. We immediately run to the Lord for help, seeking a fresh sense of His presence and power. But have you noticed? It is in the crucible of grace that we experience an inexplicable, exhilarating joy—like the sight of a distant lighthouse while traversing treacherous seas. Suddenly our closet of prayer becomes the safest sanctuary on earth. The Word of God becomes more precious than food or drink. Though faint, songs of redemption are sung from quivering lips, and despite the pain. Such a response gives testimony to the power of the Spirit who animates our hearts to "exult in our tribulations, knowing that tribulation brings about perseverance" (Rom. 5:3).

Whenever we find ourselves in some unexpected sorrow, please understand that God is not only *in* our tribulation, but that He has ordained it. We may never know the full extent of what He is doing in our life, but we can know with certainty that it is "God who is at work in [us], both to will and to work for His good pleasure" (Phil 2:13). For this reason, Paul encouraged the saints by saying, "Do not lose heart, but though our outer man is decaying, yet our inner man is being renewed day by day. For momentary, light affliction is producing for us an eternal weight of glory far beyond all comparison" (2 Cor. 4:15-17).

Charles Spurgeon offers a poignant personal testimony regarding what it is to "exult in our tribulations" when he said this:

There is a secret sweetness in the gall and wormwood of our daily trials, a sort of ineffable, unutterable, indescribable, but plainly-experienced joy in sorrow, and bliss in woe. Oh friends, I think that the happiest moments I have ever known have been just after the sharpest pains I have ever felt. As the blue gentian flower grows just upon the edge of the Alpine glacier, so, too, extraordinary joys, azure-tinted with the light of heaven, grow hard by the severest of our troubles, the very sweetest and best of our delights.[4]

Oh the blessings that are ours in Christ! But there is even more that God wants us to know. Not only does our justification provide *peace with God, access to God, a permanent standing before God, a jubilant hope of glory,* and *joy in tribulation,* but also He graciously provides *proof of our salvation.* And to that subject we now turn.

6

Proof of Salvation

> *... tribulation brings about perseverance;
> and perseverance, proven character.*
> ROMANS 5:4

There will always be some measure of mystery in suffering. Severe trials can test our faith. Even the most mature saint may begin to question God's goodness when the level of pain reaches the limits of our ability to endure.

But it is important to understand that God's purpose in suffering is not to cause us to *question* His goodness, but to *prove* it in ways we never could have imagined. God wants to demonstrate His infinite love for us in the midst of the sorrow—to literally prove to us that we are His.

How? *He empowers us to respond to suffering with an ever-increasing attitude of unwavering patience and con-*

fidence in His perfect plan. As we become more like Christ, our response to suffering becomes one of the most powerful evidences of our salvation. This amazing concept is beautifully summarized in the sixth benefit of justification, which naturally flows from the previous five: *God gives proof of salvation.*

Perseverance—the Proof of Saving Faith

We again turn our attention to Romans 5:4: "Tribulation brings about perseverance; and perseverance, proven character." The word translated "character" refers to the *tried and proven character of the justified saint.* This is what God is working toward in us right now. When we encounter a trial and respond with steadfast patience and "humble [ourselves] under the mighty hand of God" (1 Peter 5:6), then we know that He is at work in us. Our reaction proves that the righteousness of God has not only been *imputed* to us, but is also being progressively worked out within us on a day-by-day basis. God has not only declared us to be righteous (justification), but as a result, He has empowered us to live a righteous life (sanctification). Like Christ, we are committed to doing the Father's will, come what may. James assures us as follows: "Blessed is a man who perseveres under trial; for once he has been approved, he will receive the crown of life which the Lord has promised to those who love Him" (James 1:12).

Every seasoned saint will attest to the fact that God tempers the steel of our faith in the fires of adversity and shapes our character on the anvil of affliction. He not only wants us to feel the empowerment of the Holy Spirit so that we can remain steadfast in that faith, but He also wants us to manifest genuine faith as a witness to the power of His regenerating and sanctifying grace. Therefore, our perseverance is the experienced proof that we have been justified.

Four Foolish Responses to Trials

There are four ways unbelievers (and immature believers) tend to respond to trials.

ONE WAY is through *resignation*. They just resign themselves to it. It is the old English idea that says, "Keep a stiff upper lip." Or, as some of my cowboy friends would say, "Cowboy up!" or "Grin and bear it." But there is no real joy in resigning ourselves to difficult circumstances, and there is no hope that God is up to something wonderful beyond our understanding.

SECOND, some respond with *indignation*. They shake their fist in God's face. They think like Job's wife who told her suffering husband, "Why don't you just curse God and die?" Trials make that person's heart hard. They become sullen and sour. Immature believers in this category tend to disengage from the battle for the truth and try to avoid suffering for Christ. They slip into a cocoon of angry self-protection. Out of indignation toward God, they typically become cowards, people pleasers, fearing man more that God, disregarding Jesus' warning, "Woe to you, when all people speak well of you" (Luke 6:46). Yet Paul reminds us that "all who desire to live godly in Christ Jesus will be persecuted" (2 Tim. 3:12).

THIRD, others respond with *desperation*. They frantically try to find happiness somewhere to alleviate the pain. They go after drugs, alcohol, sex, or one of the many other deceptive delights Satan offers on his smorgasbord of temptations. They seek something to alleviate the pain of an unhappy, meaningless life.

FOURTH, yet others respond with *renunciation*. This is especially true in the hypocrite who follows Christ for all of the wrong reasons. This one has never truly been born again. Jesus described this man when He spoke of the gospel seed sown on the rocky places: "The man who hears the word, and immediately receives it with joy; yet he has no firm root in himself, but is only temporary, and when affliction or persecution arises because of the word, immediately he falls away" (Matt. 13:20).

A mature believer, however, does not respond to a trial with *resignation, indignation, desperation* or *renunciation*. Instead, he or she will respond with *exaltation*. This radically different response validates the genuineness of our faith because we know that our sovereign God is up to something in our life for our good and His glory, though we may not know what it is.

Three Purposes in God's Gift of Suffering

Scripture provides at least three reasons why God granted us the gracious gift of suffering for Christ's sake: (1) *to prove Himself powerful on our behalf*, (2) *to deepen our communion and trust in Christ*, and (3) *to cause us to exult in future glory*.

To be sure, God wants to do something in us through trials. He wants to strengthen us to help us persevere. So the first reason why God gives us the gift of suffering for Christ's sake is *to prove Himself powerful on our behalf*. Peter writes, "After you have suffered for a little while, the God of all grace, who called you to His eternal glory in Christ, will Himself perfect, confirm, strengthen and establish you" (1 Peter 5:9).

Recall Paul's description of his thorn in the flesh, "a messenger of Satan to buffet me—to keep me from exalting myself!" (2 Cor. 12:7). Evidently Satan had empowered some false apostle in the church to make Paul's life miserable. Paul asked the Lord three times to remove that thorn but God replied, "My grace is sufficient for you, for power is perfected in weakness" (2 Cor. 12:9). In other words, "I want to prove Myself powerful on your behalf." Paul's reaction is given in the very next verse. He says:

> Most gladly, therefore, I will rather boast about my weaknesses, that the power of Christ may dwell in me. Therefore I am well content with weaknesses, with insults, with distresses, with persecutions, with difficulties, for Christ's sake; for when I am weak, then I am strong (2 Cor. 12:9, 10).

That is what it means to exult in tribulation. Paul rejoiced knowing that God was intimately involved in his painful circumstances. The same is true for every believer. God wants to give us strength to persevere and manifest His goodness in ways we may have never seen before.

SECONDLY, He gives the gracious gift of suffering *to*

deepen our communion and trust in Christ. In James 1:2, we read, "Consider it all joy, my brethren, when you encounter various trials knowing that the testing of your faith produces endurance. And let endurance have its perfect result, that you may be perfect and complete, lacking in nothing" (James 1:3, 4).

As we rejoice in knowing that God is actually working in us, we endure the test with uncompromising faith and thus experience the soul-exhilarating power of His presence deep within our soul. And as He shapes us into the likeness of Christ, we increasingly manifest a Christlike character. It is for this reason we consider it all joy. Literally, "We calculate forward." We look beyond the trial, rejoicing in the divine purpose—"that [we] may be perfect and complete, lacking in nothing." God wants us to possess all we need to live for His glory and to enjoy the fullness of His blessing through our intimate communion with Him.

Like a candle in a cave, every saint who has ever suffered for the sake of Christ can attest to a profound awareness of the light of His presence in the midst of some dark season of life. Paul says, "Be anxious for nothing, but in everything by prayer and supplication with thanksgiving let your requests be made known to God. And the peace of God, which surpasses all comprehension, shall guard your hearts and your minds in Christ Jesus" (Phil. 4:6, 7). When tribulation comes, the justified saint not only possesses an objective peace *with* God, but also experiences a subjective peace *from* God. And, as we experience that peace, we long for more.

The psalmist says, "He who dwells in the shelter of the Most High Will abide in the shadow of the Almighty. I will say to the Lord, 'My refuge and my fortress, My God, in whom I trust!'" (Ps. 91:1, 2). The shelter and the shadow are figures that speak of protection and security. God Himself is the One in whom we must dwell and abide; and this is a permanent standing we enjoy because we are *in Christ* (2 Cor. 5:17). But it also speaks of a place in which we must choose to remain relationally as we abide in the vine of Christ through humble faith and obedience (John 15:1-10).

The figures of Psalm 91:1-2 speak strongly of the outstretched wings of the cherubim over the mercy seat above the Ark of the Covenant. They were stretched out to symbolize the protective power of our omnipotent God who ministers to those who cast themselves upon His mercy and who trust in His saving grace, and who, like Paul, "count all things to be loss in view of the surpassing value of knowing Christ" (Phil. 4:8). Those who commune with the Lord and walk closely with Him will enjoy sweet communion with the Lover of their souls as they relax under His outstretched wings.

It is important not to miss this. The justified saint is the one who exults *on account of* his tribulations because he understands the law of divine providence is weaving an infinitely glorious tapestry in which he is privileged to be a small part. With Shadrach, Meshach, and Abednego—who experienced the presence of the living Christ in the fires of Nebuchadnezzar—he can say, "there is no other God who is able to deliver in this way!" (Dan. 3:29). What an amazing thing it is to experience the presence of Almighty God while in the crucible of some fiery ordeal.

Finally, God grants us the gift of tribulation *that we might exult in future glory*. He wants us to revel in it, to be consumed with the joy of coming triumph made possible by our Savior and King whose glory should never be out of our sight. John Owen put it perfect in perspective when he said,

> On Christ's glory I would fix all my thoughts and desires, and the more I see of the glory of Christ, the more the painted beauties of this world will wither in my eyes and I will be more and more crucified to this world. It will become to me like something dead and putrid, impossible for me to enjoy.[5]

This was also at the heart of Peter's encouragement to the suffering saints of his day when he wrote, "Beloved, do not be surprised at the fiery ordeal among you, which comes upon you for your testing, as though some strange thing were happening to you" (1 Peter 4:12). In other words, "Don't act as if it were some accident that caught God by surprise, that somehow this was outside the purview of His will. Don't respond that way."

He went on to say, "But to the degree that you share the sufferings of Christ, keep on rejoicing, so that also at the revelation of His glory, you may rejoice with exultation. If you are reviled for the name of Christ, you are blessed, because the Spirit of glory and of God rests upon you" (1 Peter 4:13, 14). Then, later, he gives this exhortation with the promise: "Humble yourselves, therefore, under the mighty hand of God, that He may exalt you at the proper time, casting all your anxiety upon Him, because He cares for you" (1 Peter 5:6, 7).

What an enormous encouragement this is. The God of the universe actually cares for those He has justified. Although we may never know the full extent of what He is doing in our life, we know this that "God . . . is at work in you, both to will and to work for His good pleasure" (Phil. 2:13). His power is always manifested in our weakness. For this reason Paul—who endured unimaginable suffering for Christ—encourages us by saying, "We do not lose heart, but though our outer man is decaying, yet our inner man is being renewed day by day. For momentary, light affliction is producing for us an eternal weight of glory far beyond all comparison" (2 Cor. 4:16-17).

I pray that these marvelous benefits of justification are real to you, and that they shape your life and are the lens you look through as you behold all that happens around you and to you. If that is the case, regardless the trial, you will be able to say with the psalmist: "It is good for me that I was afflicted, that I may learn Your statutes. The law of Your mouth is better to me than thousands of gold and silver pieces" (Ps. 119:71, 72).

Now, as we make our final ascent up the golden staircase of the unmerited benefits of our justification, having contemplated our *peace with God*, our *access to God*, our *permanent standing before God*, our *jubilant hope of glory*, our *joy in tribulation*, and *proof of our salvation*, we now reach the pinnacle of blessing: *hope through a subjective awareness of the love of God*.

7

Hope through a Subjective Awareness of God's Love

. . . and hope does not disappoint, because the love of God has been poured out within our hearts through the Holy Spirit who was given to us.
ROMANS 5:5

When examining Paul's description of the benefits of justification, we can hear a crescendo of mounting blessings that concludes in thunderous exaltation, causing our heart to pound with exhilarating joy as we contemplate the glory that awaits us. But now he reveals a seventh blessing that seems to bring us back down to earth—one that speaks of a special need that every saint has, especially in days of sorrow this side of glory. Here he concludes by offering us *hope through a subjective awareness of the love of God.* Personally aware of this solemn provision, he describes it as a "hope [that] does not disappoint, because the love of God has been poured out within our hearts through the Holy Spirit who was given to us" (v. 5).

This is an astonishing statement. To fully understand it, we need to look at three things. First we need to examine the *purpose of hope*. What is the great function of this divine blessing in our life? Then we must grasp the *power of hope*. That is, what is the great engine of hope that drives it, that sustains it in our life? And then, finally, we must discern the *poison to hope*. What can rob us of the joys of hope, rendering us discouraged, defeated, and useless in service?

Remember that from the very beginning of chapter 5, Paul has shown how our salvation is eternally secure because of divine acquittal and imputed righteousness, all because of the sacrifice of the One who took our place as sinners (Rom. 3:26). This doctrine alone is more than sufficient to refute the destructive error that a person once justified can, because of sin, become *un*justified and lose his or her salvation—a cruel attack on not only the substitutionary atonement of Christ, but also His promise to love His own to the uttermost (John 13:1).

Moreover, Paul underscores the work of the Triune Godhead in our salvation. From this we understand that we have peace with God the Father through His Son, and we experience His love through the Holy Spirit who was given to us. In verse 5, Paul emphasizes the Spirit's work to give us absolute assurance that God's work of grace cannot be forfeited.

Whenever I reflect on this truth, I know that if I *could* lose my salvation I certainly *would*. I would have no hope because in myself I'm incapable of maintaining a sufficient measure of righteousness to preserve what God originally granted to me by His grace. How many rules would I have to obey? Does anybody have the list? How righteous would I have to be? How could I even measure it, especially knowing most of my sin is obscured by my flesh and falsely vindicated by a heart that is hopelessly biased in my favor? Even the sin I do see is only the tip of the iceberg. The fact is: *we can do no more to preserve our salvation than we did to gain it*. Salvation is all of grace. The same God who redeemed us by His grace secures us forever by that same grace.

The Purpose of Hope

First, notice carefully what the Spirit says regarding the *purpose of hope*. The apostle expresses this by revealing the opposite. He says, "Hope does not disappoint." The old King James Version translates it, "Hope maketh not ashamed." So, what is Paul saying here?

Before we consider this, it is important for us to define this hope. By using the definite article, he describes *the* hope—a specific hope, not just any hope. This is very important because we all know that many things we hope for don't come true. They leave us disappointed. But here, the apostle speaks of another kind of hope. This isn't just any kind of hope; this is *the* hope. This is a special, unique, one-of-a-kind hope. It is the hope first mentioned in verse 2: "hope of the glory of God."

We can rest assured that some day we will enjoy an unrestricted personal fellowship with the Triune God, and, when we do, we will be personally transformed into the glory of Christ. This hope strengthens and refines us through trials, which will never put us to shame. This hope will never disappoint.

Peter, who knew he would eventually be crucified for his faith, describes it as a "living hope through the resurrection of Jesus Christ from the dead" (1 Peter 1:3). The writer of Hebrews says, "This hope we have as an anchor of the soul, both sure and steadfast and which enters the presence behind the veil" (Heb. 6:19). Paul speaks of the "blessed hope" as the one that every saint looks for and "the glorious appearing of our great God and Savior Jesus Christ" (Titus 2:13). It is the "helmet of salvation" which protects us from the double-edged broadsword of doubt and discouragement (1 Thess. 5:8). This is the confident assurance for which we must always be ready to give a defense whenever someone asks us about "the hope that is within us" (1 Peter 3:15).

But what is the *purpose of this hope*? It is to protect us from disappointment, shame, and doubt, to encourage us in the midst of sorrow, and to give us assurance of salvation.

Paul endured enormous amounts of suffering at the hands of evil men, both inside and outside of the Church. It is estimated that about 25 percent of his missionary life was spent in prison. In the last months of his life, he languished in the disease-ridden squalor of a Roman prison. This was no prison like we might think of today. It was, in every sense of the word, a dungeon. Roman prisons were notorious for being overcrowded, damp, dark, and cold. The stench was vile beyond description. There were no toilets. Basically it was like sitting in a slimy septic tank. Men and women would be thrown in together, chained, either around the wrists or around the ankles, or even around the neck. Many times they were shackled to other prisoners. Like all prisoners, Paul would have been stripped naked and flogged before he went into the dungeon. His wounds would have been severe and untreated. His garments would have been placed back on him, becoming immediately bloodstained. And in that deplorable condition he would be left to sit, shackled in his pain. Sleep was almost impossible. We know from historical accounts that suicide and rape were rampant. Food and clean water were scarce. Often prisoners had to depend upon people outside the prison for sustenance. But it was there in that Roman dungeon that the apostle Paul faced imminent death, with virtually all of his close friends having abandoned him for fear of persecution.

Paul's second epistle to Timothy reveals that young Timothy was also prone to fear, discouragement, and depression. Yet in the agony of his dreadful prison condition, Paul encouraged Timothy to "Kindle afresh the gift of God which is in you through the laying on of my hands. For God has not given us a spirit of timidity, but of power and love and discipline. Therefore do not be ashamed of the testimony of our Lord, or of me His prisoner; but join with me in suffering for the gospel according to the power of God" (2 Tim. 1:6-9).

Paul continues in this vein in verse 12: "For this reason I also suffer these things, but I am not ashamed; for I know..." The term "know" literally means, "I am able to perceive with my senses. I can see it. I can behold it. I can feel it." Paul continues declaring what he knows: "I know whom I have believed and I am convinced that He is able to guard what I have entrusted to Him until that day."

Paul says to Timothy, "Timothy, you must not forget. We have *the* blessed hope that will never disappoint. So don't cower in fear. Don't succumb to discouragement and doubt. Don't be ashamed of the testimony of our Lord. Don't be ashamed of me, the Lord's prisoner, because God is in all of this. He is working things in and through our lives we can't even imagine that will ultimately inure to His eternal glory and our eternal joy."

If you read the history of the Church, especially the testimonies of martyrs, you quickly realize that even in the face of the most hideous forms of torture and death, they were never ashamed. They were never disappointed with the God they served. In fact, the very opposite is true. They gloried in their suffering. How could this happen? By the power of the living God, they possessed *the* hope—that blessed hope that will never disappoint.

The Power of Hope

Let's look more closely at verse 5. He says, "The love of God has been poured out within our hearts through the Holy Spirit who was given to us." Now, first, understand that he is not referring here to our love for God, but *God's love for us*. And the fuel that powers this hope is the *internal, conscious, subjective awareness of the love of God empowered by the Holy Spirit of God*.

Note that Paul says this hope has been "poured out" within our hearts. In the original language, the concept of "poured out" speaks of a gushing forth, not a trickling or trifling measure. It speaks of an abundant amount lavished upon us, a massive torrent—a flood! And in this case, it refers to *an outpouring of the love of God within our hearts*. What a joy to know that God is not stingy. He wants us to experience the super-abundant reality of His love for us so that we might never be afraid that God has forsaken us or reversed His acquittal. God wants us to know the love that is ours as a result of being eternally united to Christ.

To be sure, Christ is the object of our faith, works are the proof of our faith, and *feeling is the companion to faith*. But I fear many believers tend to disregard the emotional, subjective experience of God's love, peace, and presence. Certainly we must be careful because there are many who are ruled by their feelings. But despite that sinful proclivity, we must not think that emotion is an illegitimate part of the reality of our faith. God wants to empower us with this hope so we can experience every expression of His love in the vicissitudes of life and thereby enjoy a confident assurance that our faith will endure.

Paul says this love "has been poured out within our hearts." The awareness of His wonderful love permeates our heart and animates our will. We are empowered by the Spirit of God to fully perceive the reality of it and live victoriously as a result of it. He wants us to derive pleasure from the reality that our salvation is eternally secured by the One who first loved us and caused us to be born of Him (1 John 4:7-10).

May the Spirit of God flood your soul with His love and make real all of the promises that are yours in Christ Jesus. And then when trials come, you will be able to say with the apostle Paul, "But in all these things we overwhelmingly conquer through Him who loved us" (Rom. 8:37); and then from the heart may you joyfully sing:

The love of God is greater far
Than tongue or pen can ever tell;
It goes beyond the highest star,
And reaches to the lowest hell;
The guilty pair, bowed down with care,
God gave His Son to win;
His erring child He reconciled,
And pardoned from his sin.

Refrain
Oh, love of God, how rich and pure!
How measureless and strong!
It shall forevermore endure—
The saints' and angels' song.

When hoary time shall pass away,
And earthly thrones and kingdoms fall,
When men who here refuse to pray,
On rocks and hills and mountains call,
God's love so sure, shall still endure,
All measureless and strong;
Redeeming grace to Adam's race—
The saints' and angels' song.

Could we with ink the ocean fill,
And were the skies of parchment made,
Were every stalk on earth a quill,
And every man a scribe by trade;
To write the love of God above
Would drain the ocean dry;
Nor could the scroll contain the whole,
Though stretched from sky to sky.

—*Frederick M. Lehman*

Endnotes

1 https://www.theatlantic.com/ideas/archive/2019/09/atheism-fastest-growing-religion-us/598843/?utm_source=Albert+Mohler&utm_campaign=cc00b92ed9-EMAIL_CAMPAIGN_2019_04_08_09_12_COPY_01&utm_medium=email&utm_term=0_b041ba0d12-cc00b92ed9-309473641&mc_cid=cc00b92ed9&mc_eid=9f6453ff60

2 http://www.ccel.org/e/edwards/works2.vi.i.iii.html

3 Francis Turretin, *Institutes of Elenctic Theology* (trans. George Musgrave Giger; ed. James T. Ennison Jr.; Phillipsburg, NJ: Presbyterian & Reformed, 1994), 639-40.

4 Charles Spurgeon, *Joy In God* (sermon No. 2550), delivered at the Metropolitan Tabernacle, Newington, on Thursday evening, October 2nd, 1884.

5 https://www.goodreads.com/author/quotes/18457.John_Owen